HOLT

Elements of Language

THIRD COURSE

Think as a Writer: nteractive Writing WorkText

Writing Practice for Chapters 21–28

- Journal Warm-ups
- Writing Prompts
- Critical Thinking Mini-Lessons
- Revising and Proofreading

HOLT, RINEHART AND WINSTON

HOLT

Elements of

Language

THIRD COURSE

Think as a Writer: Interactive Writing WorkText

Writing Practice for Chapters 21–28

- Journal Warm-ups
- Writing Prompts
- Critical Thinking Mini-Lessons
- Revising and Proofreading

HOLT, RINEHART AND WINSTON

Table of Contents

Introduction: Thinking About Writing

Chapter 21: Creating a Word-Picture

PREVIEW WRITING WORKSHOP (Student Edition pp. 547–563)

Chapter 22: Expressing Your Thoughts

PREVIEW WRITING WORKSHOP (Student Edition pp. 580–595)

Table of Contents *(continued)*

Chapter 23: Exploring Similarities and Differences

PREVIEW
WRITING
WORKSHOP
(Student Edition pp. 616–631)

Chapter 24: Exploring Causes and Effects

PREVIEW
WRITING
WORKSHOP
(Student Edition pp. 652–666)

Chapter 25: Analyzing a Poem

PREVIEW
WRITING
WORKSHOP
(Student Edition pp. 686–705)

Table of Contents *(continued)*

Chapter 26: Investigating a Research Question

Chapter 27: Supporting an Opinion

Table of Contents *(continued)*

Chapter 28: Reviewing Television

PREVIEW

WRITING

WORKSHOP

(Student Edition pp. 812–830)

About This Book

Introduction: Thinking About Writing

Both **Your Writing Process** and **Strategies for Evaluating** and Revising on pages 1 and 2 are helpful guides that can be used to improve writing not only in language arts but in all subjects. Keep copies of these pages in your subject notebook and refer to them whenever you read or begin a writing assignment.

When you come across a Proofreading worksheet, use the **Guidelines for Proofreading** on page 3 to help you determine what corrections to make.

Use the **Symbols for Revising and Proofreading** on page 4 when you correct the following worksheets in this booklet:

- **Focus on Word Choice**
- **Focus on Sentences**
- **Proofreading, Grammar Link**

The Chapter Previews

At the beginning of each chapter is a Journal Warm-up. These warm-ups give you an opportunity to make a personal connection to the chapter. Vignettes and journal-writing prompts provide an easy entry into writing as you begin the chapter activities.

The Writing Workshops

For each activity in the writing process, from Writing to Proofreading, you are provided with a chart or graphic organizer format to help you plan, organize, and revise your work.

- **Prewriting** worksheets will help you work through steps before beginning to write your drafts. A writing framework will guide you through a final drafting plan.
- Additional **Writing Prompts** include career and cross-curricular writing ideas.
- A **Revising** form provides a format for analyzing a draft and identifying problems and solutions.
- **Revising Practice** provides an early, incomplete draft, which you can use to practice both elaborating and organizing.

A practice worksheet is provided for each **Mini-Lesson**, each **Focus on Word Choice** or **Focus on Sentences**, and for each **Grammar Link**.

Your Writing Process

Before You Write

Prewriting

- Choose your **topic.**
- Identify your **purpose and audience.**
- Generate **ideas** and gather **information** about the topic.
- Begin to **organize** the information.
- Draft a **sentence** that expresses your main point.

While You Write

Writing

- Grab your readers' attention in the **introduction.**
- Provide **background information.**
- State your **main points,** your **supports,** and your **elaboration** of them.
- Follow a **plan** of organization.
- Wrap up with a **conclusion.**

After You Write

Revising

- **Evaluate** your draft.
- Revise or edit the draft to improve its **content, organization,** and **style.**

After You Have Written

Publishing

- **Proofread** your final draft.
- **Publish,** or **share,** your finished writing with readers.
- **Reflect** on your writing experience.

Strategies for Evaluating and Revising

Evaluate Your Draft

- **Re-read.** Re-read your draft carefully—not once, but several times—focusing on content, organization, and style.
- **Ask.** Ask a peer to read the draft, point out weak or confusing parts, and make suggestions.

Content and Organization

- **Add.** Add sensory or factual details, examples, and illustrations.
  Add words and phrases (such as *as a result, for example, first,* and *however*) to connect ideas.
- **Delete.** Delete words, sentences, and paragraphs that stray from your thesis.
  Delete padding—unnecessary words and repetition.
- **Replace.** Replace elements that don't work as well as they should.
  Replace a weak piece of support with one that backs up your main idea more effectively.
- **Rearrange.** Rearrange sentences and paragraphs to find the clearest order of ideas.
- **Elaborate.** Elaborate and support each main point by providing specific details, facts, examples, illustrations, sensory images, figurative details, quotations, or anecdotes.

Revise for Style

- **Eliminate.** Eliminate slang, clichés, and worn-out verbs.
- **Avoid.** Avoid using the passive voice.
- **Vary.** Vary sentence length and sentence beginnings.
- **Combine.** Combine sentences to add variety or complexity.

Guidelines for Proofreading

	Yes	No	Needs Work
1. Is every sentence complete, not a fragment or run-on?			
2. Are punctuation marks—such as end marks, commas, semicolons, colons, dashes, and quotation marks—used correctly?			
3. Are the first words of sentences, proper nouns, and proper adjectives capitalized?			
4. Does every verb agree in number with its subject?			
5. Are verbs and tenses used correctly?			
6. Are subject and object forms of personal pronouns used correctly?			
7. Does every pronoun agree with its antecedent in number and in gender? Are pronoun references clear?			
8. Are frequently confused words (such as *fewer* and *less*, *affect* and *effect*) used correctly?			
9. Are all words spelled correctly? Are the plural forms of words correct?			
10. Is the paper neat and correct in form?			

Symbols for Revising and Proofreading

Symbol	Example	Meaning of Symbol
≡	Fifty-first street	Capitalize a lowercase letter.
/	Jerry's Aunt	Lowercase a capital letter.
∧	differant (e)	Change a letter.
∧	the capital Ohio (of)	Insert a missing word, letter, or punctuation mark.
∧‾	beside the river (lake)	Replace a word.
℘	Where's the the key?	Leave out a word, letter, or punctuation mark.
℘	an invisibIle guest	Leave out and close up.
⁐	a close friend ship	Close up space.
∿	thier	Change the order of letters.
(tr)	Avoid having too many corrections (of your paper) in the final version.	Transfer the circled words. (Write *tr* in nearby margin.)
¶	¶"Hi," he smiled.	Begin a new paragraph.
⊙	Stay well⊙	Add a period.
∧,	Of course you may be wrong.	Add a comma.
#	icehockey	Add a space.
(:)	one of the following(:)	Add a colon.
∧;	Maria Simmons, M.D.; Jim Fiorello, Ph.D.	Add a semicolon.
=	a great=grandmother	Add a hyphen.
∨'	Pauls car	Add an apostrophe.
(stet)	On the fifteenth of July	Keep the crossed-out material. (Write *stet* in nearby margin.)

Journal Warm-up: Descriptive Paper

Nothing—not rain, wind, or cold—can keep me away from those Friday night games. There's a special feeling in the stadium at night. For a few hours, we forget everything beyond the bright lights on the field. The band plays the fight song, and the cheerleaders leap and yell to us in the bleachers. The announcer's voice crackles with excitement with each play, and the scoreboard flashes with each touchdown.

The Japanese garden invites silence. Along the path, stone lanterns and clay pots greet visitors with a hush. A simple wooden footbridge leads over a quiet stream. On the opposite bank a bench waits for anyone listening to the water's murmurs or one's own thoughts.

JOURNAL STARTERS

Write descriptively for five minutes, using one of these prompts.

- Create a word-picture of your school building, inside or outside.
- Write a description of a nearby park during a concert.
- Describe the view from a room in your home.
- Write about your favorite place to eat.
- Describe a sporting event, such as a baseball game or a golf tournament.

NAME ______ CLASS ______ DATE ______

Evaluating Details

DIRECTIONS Evaluate the following list of details about a beach.

- Create a "short list" of the five most important details. (Remember that the details as a whole should support a **dominant impression.**)
- Answer the criteria questions about your list.
- Get together with two or three classmates and compare your results. You may not all agree on which details to include, so be prepared to explain your choices.
- Finally, revise your list.

1. sun shines golden on everything
2. shimmering sand stretches endlessly north and south
3. pretty much deserted, except on weekends or holidays
4. assorted treasures left behind by the tide—precious shells, polished stones, driftwood
5. roar of the surf drowns out other sounds
6. waves sparkle as they roll and crash
7. people fish from the piers and surf
8. tangles of seaweed on the sand glisten like necklaces
9. sunglasses and sunscreen are a must
10. good place to take a walk and be alone with your thoughts

CRITERIA

Are details included that create a clear image of the place?	Are details included that describe the location and size of the place?	Are details included to show ways in which the place is unusual?

SHORT LIST

1.
2.
3.
4.
5.

REVISED LIST

1.
2.
3.
4.
5.

Prewriting: Planning Your Description

DIRECTIONS Use the graphic organizer below to help you plan your description.

What place will you describe?	
What is your purpose?	
Who will your audience be?	
What tone will you use?	
What details, including details about your thoughts and feelings, will you use?	
What is the dominant impression you plan to convey?	
Will you use spatial order or order of importance to arrange your details?	

Writing: Writing Prompts

DIRECTIONS Choose your own topic for your descriptive paper, or use one of the following prompts.

SCHOOL

Because of an increase in the faculty and student body at your school, there are no longer enough parking spaces. The school board has proposed paving over a garden area where students often eat lunch and gather in good weather. Write a paper for the school board, describing the garden and explaining why it is important to students.

CAREERS

You are a radio news reporter. To make your reports more vivid for your listeners, you usually set the scene by describing the location of the news event. Write a paper that sets the scene for one of your reports.

LITERATURE

What places have meaning for you? Why? Write a paper that describes a place you find meaningful. Use figurative and sensory details to paint a word-picture of the place. Share your paper with a friend or a family member, or copy it in your journal.

music

Many musical compositions have been inspired by places. With the help of a music teacher or librarian, find a piece of music that evokes a place, such as Miles Davis's *Sketches of Spain*, Antonin Dvořák's *New World Symphony*, or Paul Simon's *Graceland*. Listen to the entire piece or part of it, and write a paper describing what you "see" as you listen to the music. Then, find out how you might publish your description on a music Web site.

HISTORY

Select a building in your area that is historically significant, such as a fort, the oldest building, or your city hall. Visit it, taking notes on all aspects of the building, inside and out. Then, research its history through interviews, on the Internet, or in library sources. Use the information you gather to write an interesting and detailed description of the building that could be used in a guidebook.

NAME CLASS DATE

for **CHAPTER 21: YOUR TURN 5** ***page 554***

Writing: Drafting Your Descriptive Paper

DIRECTIONS Complete the graphic organizer below, and use it to help you write your first draft. Use additional paper if necessary.

INTRODUCTION

▶ What catchy opening will you use to identify the place?

▶ How will you hint at a dominant impression?

BODY

▶ What details will you include?

▶ What thoughts and feelings will you describe?

▶ How will you place details in order?

CONCLUSION

▶ What "wrap-up" statement will you use?

NAME CLASS DATE

for **CHAPTER 21: YOUR TURN 6** page 558

Revising: Descriptive Paper

DIRECTIONS Use this chart to help you improve your descriptive paper.

QUESTIONS	DO THIS	CHANGES YOU MADE
1. Does the introduction hint at a dominant impression?	☐ **Underline** the sentence that summarizes the details.	
2. Are a variety of details (sensory, factual, and figurative) included?	☐ **Put an S** above sensory words; an **N** above numbers, and dates; and an **F** above figurative language.	
3. Are details about the writer's thoughts and feelings included?	☐ **Put an asterisk** next to every first-person pronoun *(I, me, we, us, etc.)*.	
4. Is the description clearly organized using spatial order or order of importance?	☐ **Number** the details. ☐ **Draw a map** of the place or a stair-step diagram, and place the numbers on it.	
5. Does the conclusion include a statement that wraps up the description?	☐ **Bracket** the sentence that sums up your thoughts.	

Revising Practice: Descriptive Paper

DIRECTIONS Below is an early draft of a descriptive paper.

- Revise the paper to make it more effective, using the guidelines on page 557 of your textbook.
- Look for problems with details about thoughts and feelings, variety of details, and organization.

On weekends I explore the tide pools along the shoreline. Packed with endless varieties of marine life and bustling with activity, tide pools are like miniature oceans.

Crabs move across the rocks, and schools of little fish go by.

Years of crashing ocean water has carved hollows in the rocks. Filled with water when the tide is in, these tide pools are reduced to mere puddles when the tide goes out. Despite this regular and drastic change in water level, tide pools host an amazing variety of creatures.

NAME CLASS DATE

for **CHAPTER 21: YOUR TURN 6** *page 558* **PEER- AND SELF-EVALUATION FORM**

Revising: Evaluating Descriptive Papers

DIRECTIONS Use the following questions to evaluate your descriptive paper or that of one of your classmates.

- Answer the questions.
- Rate the parts of the paper. The lowest score is 1, and the highest is 4.
- Make at least three suggestions for improving the paper.

1. What dominant impression is hinted at in the introduction?	**Rating** 1 2 3 4 ***Suggestion:***
2. Does the writer use a variety of details? What types are used?	**Rating** 1 2 3 4 ***Suggestion:***
3. What details about the writer's thoughts and feelings are provided?	**Rating** 1 2 3 4 ***Suggestion:***
4. How is the paper organized? What type of order is used?	**Rating** 1 2 3 4 ***Suggestion:***

Deadwood Adjectives

DIRECTIONS Revise the passages below by replacing deadwood adjectives that pointlessly repeat the same meaning.

- Underline the pairs of adjectives in each passage. Pairs of adjectives may be separated by a comma or joined by *and*.
- Review each pair of adjectives, and revise by replacing one of the adjectives with an adjective that adds to the meaning or by deleting the deadwood adjective.
- After you have completed this exercise, revise your paper to replace deadwood adjectives as directed in **Your Turn 7**.

PASSAGE A In the desert, where I live, people's lawns are made of sand and rock instead of grass. Some people make decorative, ornamental patterns by arranging colored gravel in their front yards. Lisa Flora, my best friend, created a realistic, lifelike flower with pink granite chips. Working together, my family wrote our address in red and crimson pebbles next to the street. Visitors often thank us for making our home so simple and easy to find. The inventive, creative arrangements on our street always attract people's attention.

PASSAGE B Although the desert seems empty and vacant, it is actually home to many kinds of plants and animals that have adapted to the uninviting and unfriendly surroundings. In severe, harsh conditions, for example, some plants can decrease the amount of water they lose. In the dry, baked environment of the desert, water obviously is needed and necessary. Plants such as cactuses have unusual and special shapes that make their surface area smaller and allow the plants to release heat easily. Various animals also have adjusted to the spare and demanding habitat of the desert. Some geckos, for instance, have webbed toes that are useful for digging in the sand and running over its loose, unstable surface.

Proofreading: Personal Pronouns

DIRECTIONS Proofread the following passages.

- Revise each incorrect pronoun. If the pronouns in a sentence are correct, write *C* following the sentence.
- After you have completed this exercise, proofread and correct the case forms of personal pronouns in your description as directed in **Your Turn 8.**

PASSAGE A On Saturday, my sister, my friend Tomás, and me visited a botanical garden. Tomás knows a lot about plants and animals. Him and my sister were fascinated by the fish they saw swimming lazily in a blue-tiled pool. Tomás told her them were *koi*. "They look like goldfish to me," she said.

"No," he answered, "they really are from the carp family. Originally the Japanese bred them for garden ponds."

"How do you suppose they feel about all we visitors wandering through their garden?" I asked. Then, us all looked closely at the orange and white fish, admiring the way the sun reflected their colors.

PASSAGE B Me and my friends love going to the state park in our area. We always stop by the mineral spring, where the water tumbles over the rocks, turning them and the soil nearby orange. The park ranger told my friends and I that the water could be contaminated and that us nature lovers should not drink from the spring. In the summer, the tall oak and maple trees and steep limestone cliffs make we feel sheltered. Many people come here because they like to rock climb. The park service encourages preserving the area by asking we hikers to stay on the trails and not litter.

Journal Warm-up: Personal Narrative

My first memory is of riding a horse. I was four years old but felt very grown-up. My father sat behind me with his arms wrapped around my waist. I clutched the horse's mane, thrilled to be high above the world!

We were taping a concert at a local TV station. I laughed when the choir director told us how to keep from fainting during the show. "Don't lock your knees while standing on the risers," she cautioned. As the concert progressed, the lights made me hot, and I began to feel nervous about my solo.

JOURNAL STARTERS

Write for five minutes about an event in your life, using one of these prompts.

- Recall a time when you had to say goodbye to a friend.
- Think of an incident that made you laugh.
- Describe your first meeting with someone.
- Remember your happiest moment.
- Describe an experience that helped you mature.

NAME _______________ CLASS _______________ DATE _______________

Prewriting: Choosing and Evaluating Topics

DIRECTIONS Use the chart below to help you choose the topic for your personal narrative.

- Write a list of memories on a separate sheet of paper, and write a one-sentence description of each memory.
- Select the two memories, or topics, that you like the most. Write the two topics at the top of the chart below.
- Complete the chart.
- Choose the topic that has the best of all four qualities in the "Questions to Consider" column.

QUESTIONS TO CONSIDER	TOPIC 1:	TOPIC 2:
Is the experience important to me? Why?		
How well do I remember the experience? List details.		
Am I willing to share the experience?		
Will my experience be interesting to others? Why?		

Prewriting: Plotting Details

DIRECTIONS After evaluating and choosing a topic in **Your Turn 4,** complete the chart below to create a plan for your personal narrative.

- After completing the chart, use a separate sheet of paper to organize the details of your narrative on a time line and write a sentence reflecting on the meaning of your experience.

Topic:

Audience:

Tone:

Purpose:

WHO OR WHAT	TRIGGER QUESTIONS	DETAILS
Events	• What is the main event in the experience? • What happened exactly? • What are some other events?	
People	• Who was in my experience? • What did they look like? • What did they say?	
Places	• Where did the experience happen? • What did the place look, sound, and smell like?	
Thoughts and Feelings	• What did I think and feel as the events unfolded?	

Using Figurative Language

DIRECTIONS On the lines below, rewrite the following sentences using a metaphor, a simile, or personification.

1. The dog played with the ball.

2. The barn was old.

3. The baseball player was quick.

4. The flowers bent in the rain.

5. I put on my worn-out football jersey.

6. The snow piled up.

7. The book smelled old.

8. The car sped down the highway.

Writing: Writing Prompts

DIRECTIONS Choose your own topic for your personal narrative, or use one of the following prompts.

Workplace

You are being interviewed for an after-school job. The interviewer asks you to describe a job that you've held before. Write a personal narrative about something interesting that happened on the job.

SCHOOL

Students are constantly being evaluated—by teachers and school administrators as well as by other students. Sometimes, students are judged on the basis of minor things, such as the clothes they wear. Other times, students are evaluated for important things, such as their performance in class. Write a personal narrative that describes a moment when you were evaluated at school.

ART

For a summer art class, you must identify a work of art that reminds you of something you have experienced. Find an appropriate work of art at the library or on the Internet. Then, write about the personal experience the work of art suggests. Be sure to include details and to explain why the experience is memorable.

PHYSICAL EDUCATION

Physical education classes often present opportunities to try new activities. You probably succeed immediately at some of these challenges and struggle with others. Write about a time when you tried a new athletic endeavor and how the experience made you feel emotionally and physically.

LITERATURE

Many personal narratives focus on adventures that a character has had. All of us have had some kind of adventure, even if it was just getting lost at the mall. Write a personal narrative about an adventure in your life.

Writing: Drafting Your Personal Narrative

DIRECTIONS Complete the graphic organizer below, and use it to help you write your first draft. Use additional paper if necessary.

INTRODUCTION

Engaging opening:

Background information:

Hint at meaning of the experience:

BODY

First event:	Second event:	Third event:
Supporting details:	Supporting details:	Supporting details:

CONCLUSION

Meaning of the experience:

NAME CLASS DATE

for **CHAPTER 22: YOUR TURN 7** *page 591*

Revising: Personal Narrative

DIRECTIONS Use the chart below to help you improve your personal narrative.

QUESTIONS	DO THIS	CHANGES YOU MADE
1. Does the opener grab attention, provide background information, and hint at the meaning of the experience?	☐ **Bracket** the attention-grabber and background information. ☐ **Underline** the hint about the meaning of the experience.	
2. Are realistic details about events, people, and places included?	☐ **Circle** details.	
3. Are there details about thoughts and feelings?	☐ **Highlight** sentences that contain thoughts or feelings.	
4. Is the order of events clear?	☐ **Number** the events in chronological order.	
5. Is the meaning of the experience discussed?	☐ **Underline** sentences in the conclusion that explain the meaning of the experience.	

for **CHAPTER 22: YOUR TURN 7** *page 591*

Revising Practice: Personal Narrative

DIRECTIONS Below is an early draft of a personal narrative.

- Revise the narrative to make it more effective, using the guidelines on page 590 in your textbook.
- Look for problems with the introduction, with the order of events, and with supporting details.

When I decided to run for class president, I considered only the difference I could make. I didn't anticipate how the campaign would affect my greatest fear.

I interviewed the debate coach, who suggested relaxation techniques. I had to give a speech to the entire ninth grade. Terrified of speaking to large groups, I resolved to conquer my fear. She said to breathe deeply and speak slowly. She also recommended finding a friend in the audience.

On stage, I sounded calm and confident, even though my knees trembled behind the podium. I survived the experience and heard positive comments from classmates. I won the election, so I'll have many chances to improve my public speaking skills.

Revising: Evaluating Personal Narratives

DIRECTIONS Use the following questions to evaluate your personal narrative or that of one of your classmates.

- Answer the questions.
- Rate the parts of the personal narrative. The lowest score is 1, and the highest is 4.
- Make at least three suggestions for improving the narrative.

1. How does the introduction grab the reader's attention, provide background information, and hint at the meaning of the experience?	**Rating** 1 2 3 4 ***Suggestion:***
2. What descriptive details are provided about events, people, and places?	**Rating** 1 2 3 4 ***Suggestion:***
3. What words does the writer use to express thoughts and feelings?	**Rating** 1 2 3 4 ***Suggestion:***
4. Why does the writer present events in this order?	**Rating** 1 2 3 4 ***Suggestion:***
5. How thoroughly is the meaning of the experience discussed?	**Rating** 1 2 3 4 ***Suggestion:***

Precise Verbs

DIRECTIONS Revise the following passages by replacing imprecise verbs with precise verbs. Choose vivid, accurate, and specific verbs.

- Cross out the imprecise verbs, and write precise verbs above them. You may delete or add other words if necessary.
- After you have completed this exercise, revise your personal narrative to replace common or overused verbs with precise ones as directed in **Your Turn 8.**

PASSAGE A I thought the Victorian-era house next door had been vacant for years. One day, I looked through an open window into the living room. I thought I would see nothing but dust, broken-down furniture, and trash. Instead, I saw in the dim light a room full of luxurious furniture. Suddenly, a sound made me move. "Why are you looking into my house?" an elderly man asked.

PASSAGE B I am great at putting things off. I stayed in bed too long this morning to make my lunch or eat breakfast, so at lunch I had to eat turkey sandwiches from the cafeteria. I did not prepare for my chorus audition this afternoon, so when the conductor told me to sing, he noticed I was making up most of the lyrics. This evening I talked with my friends instead of doing my homework; now it is eleven o'clock, and I still haven't used a book. Maybe I avoid doing things because it makes life more interesting. I know it's time to make some changes, though, because I am tired of all this excitement!

Proofreading: Subject-Verb Agreement

DIRECTIONS Proofread the following passages for subject-verb agreement with interrupting prepositional phrases.

- In the first passage, underline the correct verb in each pair provided. In the second passage, cross out and correct incorrect verb forms.
- After you have completed this exercise, revise your personal narrative to eliminate errors in subject-verb agreement as directed in **Your Turn 9.**

PASSAGE A The gym teachers at our school often (asks, ask) students to demonstrate how to hold a medicine ball without straining back muscles. Today it is my turn, and I am nervous. While the entire class of thirty students (watches, watch), I let go and the ball drops on my feet. All the students, along with the teacher, (is, are) smiling. Although I am upset about my aching toes, I am more distressed about blushing. A slight flush on the cheeks (is, are) not my problem. Instead, a sensation of increasing warmth quickly (climbs, climb) up my neck and (spreads, spread) across my face. During this embarrassing process, I feel a prickly sensation, as if the spines of a cactus (is, are) being rubbed across my skin.

PASSAGE B My sister and I, as we arrive home from school, sense something is different. Our father's pickup truck in the driveway is the first clue. Other vehicles along the curb in front of our house belongs to our relatives. We anxiously wonder why everyone at this hour are at our house. When we walk in, Dad lunges toward us and shouts, "We've won the lottery!" The two lottery tickets in his fist stands straight up like freshly minted dollar bills, but one of them is worth a lot more than a dollar! The tickets, along with a coffee pot, was a birthday present from my aunt. Everyone in the family, from Grandma to my twin toddler cousins, burst with excitement. Smiles from ear to ear adorns their faces.

for **CHAPTER 23: PREVIEW** *page 605*

Journal Warm-up: Comparison-Contrast Essay

As a native speaker of English, I found German fairly easy to learn. The two languages do have important differences, however. For instance, all nouns in German are classified as masculine, feminine, or neuter whether they refer to people or to furniture.

Both my father and I have red hair and freckles. We have the same shoe size and are almost the same height. Our similarities stop there, though. My father likes jazz, but I like rock-and-roll. He enjoys reading, while I love playing sports.

JOURNAL STARTERS

Write for five minutes, using one of these prompts.

- Compare and contrast your two favorite sports.
- Compare and contrast two trips you have taken.
- Compare and contrast two books you have read or two films you have seen.
- Compare and contrast two of your classes.
- Compare and contrast two hobbies you enjoy.

NAME CLASS DATE

Evaluating to Eliminate Irrelevant Details

DIRECTIONS Work with a partner to figure out which of the items in each list below does not belong.

- Circle the item that does not belong.
- Explain why it does not belong in the list.

1. palm trees, dandelions, ferns, toads, tumbleweeds

2. leopard, dog, cat, horse, cow

3. mountain, ocean, snow, valley, gulf, plateau, lake, island

4. a novel, a play, a poster, an essay, a short story, a biography

5. biscuits, bread, macaroni, meatloaf, pancakes, crackers, cereal

6. eyes, hair, feathers, scales, fur

7. China, India, Holland, Japan, Thailand, Vietnam, Pakistan

8. tanker, boat, canoe, rowboat, kayak, ferry, yacht

9. violin, piano, clarinet, drums, orchestra, flute, trombone, harp

10. soccer, golf, sledding, baseball, tennis

Prewriting: Organizing Ideas

DIRECTIONS Use the graphic organizer below to help you organize your ideas before you begin writing your essay.

Subjects for Comparison	**1.** **2.**
Audience and Tone	
Supporting Information	
Thesis Statement	
Features that Support Thesis Statement	**1.** **2.** **3.** **4.**
Features Organized by Point-by-Point or Block Method	

Writing: Writing Prompts

DIRECTIONS Choose your own topic for your comparison-contrast essay, or use one of the following prompts.

SCHOOL

Students' slang has changed over time. During the 1920s, for instance, a person who lacked a sense of humor was labeled "wet." Ask older family members and adults about slang expressions they used when they were about your age. Write an essay that compares and contrasts slang used today with slang used when the family member or adult was your age. Share your findings with your classmates.

CAREERS

Think of two careers that interest you. Make a list of their similarities and differences. If you need to gather information, talk to people who have experience with the careers. Then, use your list to write an essay comparing and contrasting the careers. Save your essay in a careers portfolio so you can refer to it when you are making a career plan.

MUSIC

Research two different styles of music at the library or on the Internet. Write an essay that compares and contrasts the two styles.

MATHEMATICS

How is the math that ancient Egyptians used similar to and different from the math we use today? Why was it different? Write an essay that compares and contrasts Egyptian mathematics with our current system.

SCIENCE

Different types of garbage break down, or decompose, at different rates. A newspaper, for instance, decomposes much more quickly than a plastic bag does. Identify several objects, such as sandwich bags and juice boxes, that are thrown away at your school. Then, research the amount of time it takes for each item to break down. Write an essay for your school newspaper that compares and contrasts the decomposition rates of the objects. You might include information about whether the objects can be recycled.

Writing: Drafting a Comparison-Contrast Essay

DIRECTIONS Complete the graphic organizer below, and use it to help you write your first draft.

INTRODUCTION

- How will you capture your readers' attention?
- What background information will you provide?
- What is your thesis?

BODY

- Will you organize your information using the block or point-by-point method?

CONCLUSION

- How does your supporting information lead to your thesis?
- How will you bring your essay to a close?

NAME CLASS DATE

Revising: Comparison-Contrast Essay

DIRECTIONS Use this chart to help you improve your comparison-contrast essay.

QUESTIONS	DO THIS	CHANGES YOU MADE
1. Do the first sentences grab the audience's attention?	☐ **Put a check** above the interesting parts of first one or two sentences. If you see no check marks, revise.	
2. Does the introduction clearly identify both subjects and the thesis of the essay?	☐ **Draw a squiggly line** under each subject. ☐ **Underline** the thesis.	
3. Is the body organized by the block method or the point-by-point method?	☐ **Write *A*** above each point about the first subject. ☐ **Write *B*** above each point about the second subject.	
4. Does the conclusion bring the essay to a definite close by summarizing or evaluating the subjects?	☐ **Underline** sentences that summarize and evaluate. If there aren't any, revise.	

for **CHAPTER 23: YOUR TURN 6** **page 628**

Revising Practice: Comparison-Contrast Essay

DIRECTIONS Below is an early draft of a comparison-contrast essay.

- Revise the essay to make it more effective, using the guidelines on page 627 of your Student's Edition.
- Look for ways to improve the introduction, the thesis, and supporting information.

Trains can be a good form of transportation. Maglev trains offer an attractive alternative to traditional railroads. Most regular train locomotives are powered by diesel fuel and run on two steel rails fastened to crossties made of wood or concrete. Magnetic levitation (maglev) trains, however, have no wheels and float over a track. They are powered by an electrical device that creates a magnetic field between the track and the train. If maglev trains were used more widely, there would probably be fewer passenger deaths.

This advanced technology allows the maglev to move much faster than traditional locomotives do. Regular trains travel at about ninety miles per hour. The maglev, however, cannot derail, and it cannot collide with or overtake another train from behind.

DATA

- Maglev trains average about three hundred miles per hour.
- A regular train collides with a person or vehicle about every one hundred minutes in the United States.
- Russia has the longest rail line in the world.

NAME CLASS DATE

Revising: Evaluate Comparison-Contrast Essays

DIRECTIONS Use the following questions to evaluate your comparison-contrast essay or that of a classmate.

- Answer the questions.
- Rate the parts of the essay. The lowest score is 1, and the highest is 4.
- Make at least three suggestions for improving the essay.

1. What grabs the audience's attention in the first one or two sentences?	**Rating** 1 2 3 4 ***Suggestion:***
2. How does the introduction identify both subjects and the thesis of the essay?	**Rating** 1 2 3 4 ***Suggestion:***
3. In what ways does the body organization show either the block method or the point-by-point method?	**Rating** 1 2 3 4 ***Suggestion:***
4. How effective is the conclusion in bringing the essay to a close through summary or evaluation?	**Rating** 1 2 3 4 ***Suggestion:***

NAME ______________________ CLASS ______________________ DATE ______________________

Varying Sentence Length

DIRECTIONS Revise the following passage by combining closely related sentences. Make changes within the passage, as shown in the first sentence.

- Reduce some sentences to phrases, and insert them into other sentences. You may delete or add words if necessary.
- After you have completed this exercise, revise your essay to vary sentence length as directed in **Your Turn 7.**

Magical Rainbows

You've probably seen a rainbow/ ~~You've probably seen a rainbow~~ created by the sun. Other rainbows are a much rarer sight. These other rainbows are produced by moonlight. These magical nighttime bands of color are fainter than rainbows people see during the day. They are fainter because moonlight is not as bright as sunlight. In other ways, however, traditional rainbows and moonlight rainbows are very similar.

Both kinds of rainbow are created when light hits water droplets. These water droplets are suspended in the air. If the light reflects into your eyes at a certain angle, you see a rainbow. To get the best view of a rainbow, you need to stand with the sun or the moon behind you. When the sun or moon is behind you, its light hits the droplets. The light then reflects back toward you.

Both kinds of rainbow also involve sunlight. They both involve sunlight since moonlight is actually sunlight reflected off the moon. Both rainbows also are made up of the standard seven colors. The standard rainbow colors are red, orange, yellow, green, blue, indigo, and violet. Both rainbows also include colors the eye cannot see.

NAME CLASS DATE

Correcting Misplaced Modifiers

DIRECTIONS Revise the following passages, correcting any misplaced participial phrases used as modifiers. Make your changes within the passages, as shown in the first sentence.

- You may add or delete punctuation; capitalize or lowercase letters; and change, add, or delete words as necessary.
- After you have completed this exercise, revise your essay to correct any misplaced modifiers as directed in **Your Turn 8.**

PASSAGE A My parents finally agreed that I could get a pet tired of my pestering. It was up to me to decide between a dog and a cat. My first thought was to get a dog knowing how intelligent dogs are. However, needing to be walked several times a day, I would not always be home to take care of a pet. Trained to use a litter box, my friend suggested it might be more convenient to have a cat. I still wanted a dog longing for companionship. However, living in the house instead of outdoors, my friend convinced me that a cat would be as good a companion as a dog.

PASSAGE B Here's my dilemma. I need to choose between two activities. Auditioning for a play and trying out for soccer, both the theater arts director and the soccer coach have urged me to become more involved. I would exercise my mind learning a part in a play. Scheduled for just the month of September, I see other advantages to being in the play. On the other hand, I would have no other activities the rest of the season working on the play for only a month. However, I would have practice and compete in games being part of the soccer team all fall. I would exercise my body playing soccer regularly. I think physical exercise is what I need most this semester. I think I will try out for the team offered the choice.

Journal Warm-up: Cause-and-Effect Explanation

The plane crash was caused by ice buildup on the wings. One effect was an immediate policy change issued to all pilots and ground crews. Now, all planes are de-iced ten minutes before takeoff.

The movie shows every Friday at midnight to a sellout crowd. Five years ago, when it closed after a twelve-week run, students picketed the theater, letters appeared in all the newspapers, and a petition with two thousand signatures was presented to theater management. As a result, the movie is now shown every week.

JOURNAL STARTERS

Write for five minutes about causes and effects, using one of these prompts.

- Describe the effects of something you did recently.
- How might the weather affect your plans for the weekend?
- Discuss the causes of a team's win or loss.
- How does too little or too much sleep affect you?
- Are you ever late for school? Why?

Prewriting: Organizing Ideas for Your Topic

DIRECTIONS Use the graphic organizer below to help you choose a topic for your essay and begin to plan it.

BRAINSTORM AND LIST

NARROW TOPIC

CONSIDER YOUR READERS

What they already know:	What they will need to know:

STATE MAIN IDEA (THESIS)

GATHER SUPPORT

Causes or Effects	Support

False Cause and Effect

DIRECTIONS Determine whether each of the following sentences contains a false cause-and-effect relationship.

- Write *F* after any passage that contains a false cause-and-effect relationship, and write *OK* after any passage that expresses a valid relationship.
- Briefly explain your choice in the space below each passage.

1. If the downtown developers would only build a performing arts center, then everybody would come back downtown to shop. ______

2. Benito and I planned to go to the mall on Saturday, but now Benito can't go. He's visiting some relatives instead. ______

3. One of the judges for the gold medal judo match was from the United States. The athlete who won the match was also from the United States. Obviously, he won because he and the judge were from the same country. ______

4. The new film *Whiskers* was nominated for four Academy Awards. As a result, ticket sales almost doubled on the following weekend. ______

5. Cass and I must have been watching the same quiz show last night. I heard her use the word *oligarchy* this morning; it was one of the clues in the show. ______

6. The TV show "Creatures of the Night" was canceled after only one season. The actors probably got bored. ______

Writing: Writing Prompts

DIRECTIONS Choose your own topic for your cause-and-effect explanation, or use one of the following prompts.

WORKPLACE

Your employer has announced that anyone who does not carpool will have to pay $25 a month for parking. What do you think caused your company to make such a rule? Write a cause-and-effect explanation of the effects (positive or negative) that you think this policy will have on employees' attitudes and behaviors.

SCHOOL

Your school has decided that the school dress code should be expanded to regulate what kinds of jewelry are acceptable to wear to school. Write a cause-and-effect explanation of the effects the proposed "jewelry rule" would have on students.

JOURNALISM

Technology allows photographs to be altered to substitute one person's face for another, to change backgrounds, and to create many different effects. Some newspapers have made a promise that they will not publish altered photographs. What might some causes be for creating this policy? Write a cause-and-effect explanation of this subject.

HISTORY

New information often causes people to view history differently. For example, the diary of a Mexican soldier who served under Santa Anna reported that Davy Crockett and others at the Alamo were executed after surrendering. This changed some traditional views of the battle. Imagine that a significant piece of new information has been discovered about a historical event you have studied recently. Write a cause-and-effect explanation of possible effects of this discovery.

SCIENCE

Thousands of species of animals on Earth are endangered: they are expected to disappear in less than 20 years if special measures are not taken to protect them. Select an endangered animal, and write a cause-and-effect explanation showing why the animal is endangered and what might happen if the animal becomes extinct.

Writing: Drafting a Cause-and-Effect Explanation

DIRECTIONS Use the graphic organizer below to outline your explanation or make notes. After you have completed the organizer, use it to write your draft. Use additional paper if necessary.

INTRODUCTION

▶ How will you grab your readers' attention?

▶ What background information about causes and effects will you provide?

▶ What is your thesis?

BODY

▶ What is your first cause or effect?

What support will you use?

▶ What is your second cause or effect?

What support will you use?

▶ What is your third cause or effect?

What support will you use?

CONCLUSION

▶ How will you wrap up and restate your thesis?

Revising: Cause-and-Effect Explanation

DIRECTIONS Use this chart to help you improve your cause-and-effect explanation.

QUESTIONS	DO THIS	CHANGES YOU MADE
1. Will the introduction quickly interest readers in the event or situation?	☐ **Circle** sentences in the introduction that you think will interest readers.	
2. Is there a clear thesis that shows the focus of the essay—either causes or effects?	☐ **Underline** the thesis statement twice.	
3. Are causes and effects supported with evidence?	☐ **Circle** each sentence that offers support.	
4. Is the information for each cause or effect clear and easy to follow?	☐ **Number** causes and effects in sequence. ☐ **Underline** the most important cause or effect.	
5. Does the conclusion include a restatement of the focus of the explanation?	☐ **Circle** the sentence in the conclusion that restates the focus.	

Revising Practice: Cause-and-Effect Explanation

DIRECTIONS Below is an early draft of a cause-and-effect explanation.

- Revise the paper to make it more effective, using the guidelines on page 661.
- Look for problems with the introduction, thesis statement, and supporting evidence.

After my grandmother had her hip replacement surgery, she came to stay with us while she recovered. I knew my mom would spend more time helping Grandma, but that did not bother me. What did worry me was giving up my room and moving in with my little brother. He didn't seem to mind, since all he wants to do is follow me around anyway. I could see it was going to be trouble.

However, Charlie turned out to be a fine roommate. I was actually sorry to see my Grandma return to her home. Her surgery helped me get to know my brother better.

Revising: Evaluating Cause-Effect Explanations

DIRECTIONS Use the following questions to evaluate your cause-and-effect explanation or that of one of your classmates.

- Answer the questions.
- Rate the parts of the explanation. The lowest score is 1, and the highest is 4.
- Make at least three suggestions for improving the explanation.

1. How does the introduction get readers' attention?	**Rating** 1 2 3 4 ***Suggestion:***
2. What is the thesis?	**Rating** 1 2 3 4 ***Suggestion:***
3. Find at least one piece of evidence that supports each cause or effect.	**Rating** 1 2 3 4 ***Suggestion:***
4. Which cause or effect is easiest to understand? Which is hardest to follow?	**Rating** 1 2 3 4 ***Suggestion:***
5. How does the conclusion restate the focus of the explanation?	**Rating** 1 2 3 4 ***Suggestion:***

Varied Beginnings

DIRECTIONS Use the three strategies to vary sentence beginnings. Write your revisions in the space after the paragraph, or use your own paper if necessary. After you have completed this exercise, revise your essay to improve your sentence beginnings as directed in **Your Turn 7.**

PASSAGE A Students often find the move from middle school to high school difficult. They think more may be expected of them in high school. They feel that they may not be prepared. Furthermore, they worry about being accepted by the older students in the high school. These older students often include their own brothers and sisters.

REVISION

STRATEGIES YOU USED

- ☐ **Reword or reorder for variety.**
- ☐ **Combine sentences.**
- ☐ **Add transitions.**

PASSAGE B The state legislature recently passed a law that all high school students must complete twenty hours of volunteer service each school year. Lawmakers think the schools need to teach students about the community as well as to teach students academic subjects. The legislature fears that students will not be good citizens if they do not consider the needs around them.

REVISION

STRATEGIES YOU USED

- ☐ **Reword or reorder for variety.**
- ☐ **Combine sentences.**
- ☐ **Add transitions.**

Proofreading: Inexact Pronoun Reference

DIRECTIONS Proofread and correct the following passages by correcting the inexact pronoun references. After you have completed this exercise, turn to the draft of your explanation and complete **Your Turn 8.**

PASSAGE A When the men at the 1840 London World Anti-Slavery Convention refused to allow women delegates to be seated, they were very angry. Two of them from the United States—Lucretia Mott, from Pennsylvania, and Elizabeth Cady Stanton, from New York—pledged to work for the rights of women. Mott and Stanton called the first women's rights convention in her hometown, Seneca Falls, New York. Both women were writers and public speakers for the rights of blacks and women. They had very few legal rights during the late nineteenth century. Stanton convinced a U.S. senator to sponsor an amendment for woman suffrage in 1878. They finally passed the bill in 1919.

PASSAGE B Inventor Percy Spencer had a chocolate bar in his pocket as he toured the laboratories at his company, Raytheon. While standing in front of a machine called a magnetron, he noticed that it began to melt. He told a colleague that he needed some unpopped popcorn. When he held each kernel to the magnetron, it exploded. After this experiment, Spencer developed the first commercial-use microwave ovens, which were over five feet tall and weighed 750 pounds. They continued working on the technology for home use. When Raytheon bought Amana Refrigeration, they finally had the technology to produce countertop microwaves.

Journal Warm-up: Analysis of a Poem

Your class has been reading and discussing poems by Emily Dickinson. You recently read a poem called "Apparently with no surprise," and a classmate is confused by a line that reads "The blonde Assassin passes on—." You think you know what it means, but you decide to analyze the poem to make sure your interpretation makes sense.

Life is compared to the theater in "The Seven Ages of Man," by William Shakespeare. According to the speaker, the world is a stage, and we are just actors who come and go. Our lives are broken into seven acts, or "ages," beginning with infancy and extending to a "second childishness" in old age.

JOURNAL STARTERS

Write analytically for five minutes, using one of the prompts below.

- Summarize your favorite song or rap, and explain its meaning.
- Interpret a nursery rhyme you remember.
- Explain the images in a state or national song.
- Why do you like or dislike a particular poem?
- Explain the meaning of a proverb or wise saying.

Prewriting: Choosing and Analyzing a Poem

DIRECTIONS Use the analysis log below to help you analyze a poem.

- Choose a poem, and write down your first thoughts about it on a separate piece of paper.
- Copy the poem in the left-hand column of your log.
- Write your notes about the literary elements of the poem in the right-hand column.

ANALYSIS LOG

Poem title: ______ Author: ______	NOTES

Sound Elements in Poetry

DIRECTIONS For each passage below, identify
a. each word that contains any of the sound elements described on page 691
b. the type of sound elements
c. how you think the sound elements add to the meaning of the passage

Since you are given only a few lines of each poem, examine *the title* of each poem for hints about meaning.

Passage	a.	b.	c.
...I wandered off by myself, In the mystical moist night air, and from time to time, Looked up in perfect silence at the stars. —Walt Whitman, "When I Heard the Learn'd Astronomer"			
When all at once I saw a crowd, A host, of golden daffodils Beside the lake, beneath the trees, Fluttering and dancing in the breeze. —William Wordsworth, "I Wandered Lonely as a Cloud"			
They all hiss as they glide, like inches, down the marked tapes. Those soft shapes, shadowy inside the hard bodies—are they their guts or their brains? —May Swenson, "Southbound on the Freeway"			
...I love them for ... wanting to know it, for assuming there is such a secret, yes, for that most of all. —Denise Levertov, "The Secret"			

Prewriting: Thesis, Support, and Organization

DIRECTIONS Use the graphic organizer below to write your thesis, gather and explain your supporting evidence, and organize your essay.

WRITING A THESIS

Title and Poet:

Poetic Elements:

Statement of Meaning or Theme:

Thesis Statement:

GATHERING SUPPORT

Element	Detail or Quotation	Explanation

ORGANIZING

Thesis:

Most important idea:	**Explain**
Second most important idea:	**Explain**
Third most important idea:	**Explain**

Writing: Writing Prompts

DIRECTIONS Choose your own poem for your analysis, or use one of the following prompts.

CAREERS

You are working on posters for a job fair and would like to include some inspirational quotations. Search a poetry collection for lines from a poem that might help motivate a person your age who is looking for a job or thinking about career paths. When you have identified an appropriate selection from a poem, explain its meaning. Ask your language arts teacher if you have correctly interpreted the selection.

SCHOOL

Most schools use cheers to build school spirit and show support for sports teams and other groups. Cheers are often poems of a sort, containing rhymes, imagery, and other poetic elements. For your school newspaper, analyze one of your school's cheers.

MUSIC

Many folk songs are poems set to music. At the library, on the World Wide Web, or with the help of a music teacher, find a folk song that interests you. Copy the words of the song on a piece of paper. Then, write an analysis of the song's meaning and share it with your classmates.

SOCIAL STUDIES

Poems reveal a great deal about people's lives and times. Search poetry collections in the library or on the World Wide Web for poems about other places and times. Choose a poem that appeals to you. Then, write about what the poem means to you and what insights it gives you into a different place and time.

MATHEMATICS

Haiku is a form of poetry that follows specific rules for number of syllables and lines. Research the rules that govern haiku. Then, select a haiku, and write a paragraph explaining how the form of the poem contributes to its meaning. Share your ideas with others in your class.

NAME ______ CLASS ______ DATE ______

for **CHAPTER 25: YOUR TURN 6** ***page 696***

Writing: Drafting an Analysis of a Poem

DIRECTIONS Complete the graphic organizer below, and use it to help you write your first draft. Use additional paper if necessary.

INTRODUCTION

▶ What statement will you use to relate the poem's meaning to a common human experience?

▶ What is the title? Who is the author?

▶ What is your thesis statement?

BODY

▶ What is the first key poetic element?

▶ What is the second key poetic element?

▶ What is the third key poetic element?

CONCLUSION

▶ How will you restate the thesis and the poem's broader themes?

Revising: Analysis of a Poem

DIRECTIONS Use this chart to help you improve the analysis of your poem.

QUESTIONS	DO THIS	CHANGES YOU MADE
1. Are the author and title named in the introduction?	☐ **Highlight** the title and the author.	
2. Does the introduction have a clear thesis and include key poetic elements?	☐ **Underline** the thesis statement. ☐ **Circle** the poetic elements.	
3. Does each body paragraph contain a clear main idea that supports the thesis?	☐ **Bracket** the key poetic element discussed in each body paragraph.	
4. Is the main idea of each body paragraph well supported with evidence and explanations?	☐ **Draw a box** around supporting quotations or details. ☐ **Draw a wavy line** under elaboration and explanations.	
5. Does the conclusion remind readers of the thesis and close the essay?	☐ **Highlight** the sentence that restates the thesis.	

NAME CLASS DATE

Revising Practice: Analysis of a Poem

DIRECTIONS Below is an early draft of an analysis of a poem.

- Revise the analysis to make it more effective, using the guidelines on page 700.
- Look for problems with the introduction, thesis, and key poetic elements.

This tight little poem takes on a subject of great importance to all human beings: the end of the world. The speaker weighs two theories about how we will perish—by fire or by ice.

The speaker carefully repeats vowel sounds. The long *i* sound is repeated, for example, at the end of all lines except 6 and 8. These sound effects draw our attention to the speaker's strong choice of words ("perish," "hate," "destruction" in lines 5–7) and equally strong opinions about human flaws.

The speaker uses an implied metaphor to identify fire and ice with the human emotions of desire and hate (lines 3–6). Fire and ice represent ways humans may destroy Earth.

DATA

Fire and Ice
by Robert Frost
Some say the world will end in fire,
Some say in ice.
From what I've tasted of desire
I hold with those who favor fire.
But if it had to perish twice,
I think I know enough of hate
To say that for destruction ice
Is also great
And would suffice.

Revising: Evaluating an Analysis of a Poem

DIRECTIONS Use the following questions to evaluate your analysis of a poem or that of one of your classmates.

- Answer the questions.
- Rate the parts of the analysis. The lowest score is 1, and the highest is 4.
- Make at least three suggestions for improving the analysis.

1. How does the introduction tell you about the author and title of the poem?	**Rating** 1 2 3 4 ***Suggestion:***
2. How clear is the thesis, and what key poetic elements are introduced?	**Rating** 1 2 3 4 ***Suggestion:***
3. What is the main idea of each body paragraph, and how does it support the thesis?	**Rating** 1 2 3 4 ***Suggestion:***
4. What kinds of evidence and explanations are used to support the main idea of each body paragraph?	**Rating** 1 2 3 4 ***Suggestion:***
5. How does the conclusion remind readers of the thesis and bring the essay to a close?	**Rating** 1 2 3 4 ***Suggestion:***

NAME CLASS DATE

for **CHAPTER 25: FOCUS ON SENTENCES** page 702 **PRACTICE**

Revising Wordy Sentences

DIRECTIONS Revise wordy sentences in the passages below by deleting unnecessary relative pronouns and *be* verbs.

- Reduce clauses that begin with *which is, which are, that is, that are, who is,* and *who are* to participles or participial phrases. If necessary, rearrange the remaining participles or participial phrases so that they are close to the words they modify.
- After you have completed this exercise, revise your essay to eliminate wordy sentences as directed in **Your Turn 8.**

PASSAGE A The poem "The Girl Who Loved the Sky," by Anita Endrezze, describes the tender friendship of two young girls who are left out of the friendly circle that is formed by others. The girls are different from the rest: one has "no father" and the other has "no eyes." Together on the playground swings, the two soar far above the others and share their deepest feelings. The "formless sky," which is loved by the blind girl for its taste of "cold metal" and is "defined" for her "only by sounds," welcomes the two friends and becomes a metaphor for the world that is shared by them.

PASSAGE B In A. E. Housman's poem "Smooth Between Sea and Land," the sea represents death, the land stands for birth, and the smooth sand that is between them symbolizes life. The speaker explains that waves flatten a child's mound of sand and wipe away two names that were scribbled by a teenager on the shore. He wonders whether death will erase everything he builds or writes in an attempt to achieve fame that is lasting. The speaker, who is worried, thinks he might "hold the bursting wave" back by constructing a city that is huge or by making his name famous. However, he concludes that cities are "not built to last" and "charms" that are false and used to obtain fame are pointless. Everything, he realizes, is erased by the sea of death, which is mysterious.

Proofreading: Using and Punctuating Quotations

DIRECTIONS Proofread the following passages.

- Add quotation marks and other punctuation marks where necessary in each of the following passages.
- After you have completed this exercise, revise your essay to correct quotation marks and other punctuation marks as directed in **Your Turn 9**.

PASSAGE A In John Masefield's poem "Night on the Downland, the rich, exciting past of a moorland is compared to its barren, "lonely" present: The moorland is Dark now and haunted by the moorland fowl; None comes here now but the peewit only,/And moth-like death in the owl." A gale beats the grass down and makes "wind-withered" shrubs moan "like old men. In contrast, the moorland's past was dramatic. A beautiful Roman woman lived on the "wind-barren" land. This "Lonely Beauty . . . was here in sadness, Brave as a thought on the frontier of the mind. She thought of Julius Caesar "in the purple; that is, she dreamed of him becoming king. However, Caesar was killed because his peers feared that he would crown himself. The beautiful woman disappeared, and the moorland returned to its wild, vacant state.

PASSAGE B The poet Anne Bradstreet uses a clever extended metaphor in her poem "The Author to Her Book. The speaker claims that a book she wrote is a "brat" who is "irksome in my sight." The frustrated speaker protests that the book/child insists on staying with her after its birth. If the book/child calls for her attention, she can hardly bear to respond. Over time, she tries to improve the book/child: "I washed thy face, but more defects I saw, And rubbing off a spot still made a flaw. (When the author tries to revise her book, she creates more problems.) The speaker finally gives up improving her book/child and decides to send it into the "critic's hands (publication). However, she worries that someone might wonder about the irresponsible parents of the book/child. (Will a reader ask, Who dared to publish this imperfect book?) She instructs the book/child to answer that its mother "is poor, Which caused her thus to send thee out of door.

Taking the Essay Part of a Writing Test

DIRECTIONS The graphic organizer below will help you generate ideas for an essay on an English test.

- Choose one of the writing prompts below.
- Complete the graphic organizer for the prompt.

PROMPTS

- It is often observed that "knowledge is power." Write an essay explaining what you think this quotation means. To illustrate and support your ideas, cite examples from real life, books, movies, music, or television.
- The ancient Greek philosopher Zeno is said to have described a friend as "another I." Using examples from real life, books, movies, music, or television as support, write an essay explaining what you think Zeno meant.

STEP 1: What are the important words in the prompt?

STEP 2: What are you being asked to explain or show?

STEP 3: What does the quotation mean to you?

STEP 4: What *5W-How?* questions would you ask about ideas in the prompt?

Who?	What?	When?	Where?	Why?	How?

STEP 5: How would you answer these questions?

Journal Warm-up: I-Search Paper

A friend suggested that my name, Thora, might have some connection with Thor, the Norse thunder god. That inspired me to investigate the origins of my name.

I had an attack of the hiccups in study hall yesterday, and they sounded even worse than they were. Drinking water didn't help, nor did holding my breath. I decided to do some research on what causes hiccups and how to control them.

JOURNAL STARTERS

Write for five minutes, using one of the prompts below.

- Choose a natural occurrence, such as earthquakes or tornadoes, and write five questions you have about its causes or effects.
- Guess, or write what you already know, about the origins of an item you use every day.
- Describe a place you would like to know more about.
- What kinds of music do you think led to contemporary types of music?
- Describe a sport you have seen but would like to understand better.

NAME CLASS DATE

Prewriting: Plan Your I-Search Paper, Part One

DIRECTIONS Use the graphic organizer below to plan your I-Search paper.

Topic

Research Question

Group Feedback

Audience:	Purpose:	Tone:	Voice:

Search Journal

Date:	Research Successes/ Setbacks:	Thoughts on My Progress:

NAME CLASS DATE

for **CHAPTER 26: YOUR TURN 5** ***page 737***

Prewriting: Plan Your I-Search Paper, Part Two

DIRECTIONS Use the following graphic organizer to continue planning your I-Search paper.

SOURCE EVALUATION

Source	Date	Reason I think it is factual	Reason I think it is objective	Use
				☐ Card made ☐ Notes taken
				☐ Card made ☐ Notes taken
				☐ Card made ☐ Notes taken
				☐ Card made ☐ Notes taken
				☐ Card made ☐ Notes taken
				☐ Card made ☐ Notes taken

THESIS:

INFORMAL OUTLINE

Story of my search	Results of my search	Reflections on my search

Evaluating Web Sources

DIRECTIONS Use the following chart to help you evaluate Web sites.

- Identify three Web sites you used in researching your I-Search paper.
- Answer the questions in the chart for each Web site.

	WEB SITE 1:	WEB SITE 2:	WEB SITE 3:
Coverage: How much information is provided? Is the information available from a more accessible source? If yes, name the source. If no, explain why.			
Accuracy: Could you confirm the accuracy of the information by finding the same information in another source? If yes, name the source. If no, explain.			
Currency: Is the information up-to-date? Why or why not?			
Authority: Is the author of the Web site qualified to write on the topic? Why or why not?			
Objectivity: Does the Web site present both sides of an issue?			

Writing: Writing Prompts

DIRECTIONS Choose your own topic for your I-Search paper, or use one of the following prompts.

CAREERS

You enjoy doing almost anything on the computer and have strong computer skills. You would like to find out about career opportunities in the field. What do you already know about careers in computers? What questions do you have? Where would you go to find answers to your questions? Write an I-Search paper about your investigation, including information about different sources and what you learned from them.

SCHOOL

Your school's athletic department is considering adding the sport of lacrosse next year. Although you've never participated in organized sports, this one sounds kind of interesting. What kinds of sources could you consult to learn more about lacrosse? How could you learn about the history of lacrosse? Investigate the sport, and write an I-Search paper about your research process and results. Share the paper with your friends who are also interested in lacrosse.

MUSIC

You've been taking guitar lessons for several years and have always thought you wanted to play rock music. However, you recently went to a bluegrass festival where your guitar instructor was playing and decided you really liked the sound of the banjo. Your instructor suggests you do some research about the history of the banjo and bluegrass music before deciding whether to study the banjo. Write an I-Search paper describing how you researched the topics and what you learned. Ask your instructor to read the paper.

SCIENCE

Last night on the news, the meteorologist predicted that air pollution would be bad for the next few days because a thermal inversion is trapping pollution in the area where you live. You've noticed that the sky is often yellowish brown for days, and you'd like to know more about how thermal inversions contribute to the pollution problem. Do some research on thermal inversions, and write an I-Search paper about your research and the results of your research. Share the paper with your science class.

GOVERNMENT

You have become interested in an upcoming election in your state. One candidate is using extremely negative TV advertisements against her opponent. You've decided to try to determine how many of the negative claims are true. Investigate the claims using as many sources as possible, and write an I-Search paper that explains how you conducted your research and what you found out. Share the paper with people you know who are interested in the election.

NAME CLASS DATE

Writing: Drafting Your I-Search Paper

DIRECTIONS Outline your I-Search paper or make notes, using the following organizer. After you have completed the organizer, use it to write your first draft.

THE SEARCH STORY

Attention-getting statement:

What you knew already:

What you wanted to know:

Thesis:

Steps you took:

1 __________

2 __________

3 __________

4 __________

THE SEARCH RESULTS

Result:

Result:

Result:

Result:

SEARCH REFLECTIONS

Effects of research experience:

Restatement of thesis:

NAME CLASS DATE

Revising: I-Search Paper

DIRECTIONS Use this chart to help you improve your I-Search paper.

QUESTIONS	DO THIS	CHANGES YOU MADE
1. Does the thesis answer the research question?	☐ **Underline** the thesis statement. ☐ **Box** the research results.	
2. Is the search story in logical order?	☐ **Number** each step in the order it happened.	
3. Are search results supported by information from outside sources?	☐ **Circle** major results of the search. ☐ **Underline** information from outside sources.	
4. Are enough recent, reliable, and objective print and nonprint sources used?	☐ **Highlight** information taken from the note cards.	
5. Does the conclusion tell how the research experience affected the writer?	☐ **Bracket** sentences that describe effects.	
6. Is the *Works Cited* list complete and correctly formatted?	☐ **Put a check mark** beside parenthetical citations with correctly formatted entries in the *Works Cited* list.	

Revising Practice: I-Search Paper

DIRECTIONS Below is an early draft of an I-Search paper.

- Revise the paper to make it more effective, using the guidelines on Student Edition page 749.
- Look for problems with a hook, why the writer wanted to know about the topic, and a thesis statement.

I recently watched a TV show about elephants that paint. At a special school in Thailand, elephants are trained to create abstract artwork with their trunks. That's when I realized I had an interesting research question: What animals can create art?

My search began at the library, where I found articles in the *New York Times* and in *Esquire* magazine about the school for elephant artists. I then interviewed our veterinarian, who warned me to use nontoxic paints for Mouser's artistic debut, because cats lick their paws frequently. The World Wide Web offered several sites about animals that paint, including one that exhibits paintings of cat artists!

Revising: Evaluating I-Search Papers

DIRECTIONS Use the following questions to evaluate your I-Search paper or that of one of your classmates.

- Answer the questions.
- Rate the parts of the paper. The lowest score is 1, and the highest is 4.
- Make at least three suggestions for improving the paper.

1. How does the thesis statement answer the research question?	**Rating** 1 2 3 4 ***Suggestion:***
2. In what order are the steps of the search presented?	**Rating** 1 2 3 4 ***Suggestion:***
3. What outside sources are used to support the search results?	**Rating** 1 2 3 4 ***Suggestion:***
4. How many print and nonprint sources does the writer use, and how recent, reliable, and objective are they?	**Rating** 1 2 3 4 ***Suggestion:***
5. What does the conclusion tell you about how the research experience affected the writer?	**Rating** 1 2 3 4 ***Suggestion:***
6. How complete and correct is the *Works Cited* list?	**Rating** 1 2 3 4 ***Suggestion:***

Eliminating "There is/There are" Beginnings

DIRECTIONS Revise the passages below by eliminating *there is, there are, there was,* and *there were* at the beginning of sentences. Make your changes within the passages, as shown in the first passage.

- In each sentence beginning with a *there* phrase, replace *there* with the subject of the sentence. Reword the sentence as needed. Use lively verbs whenever you can in the revised sentences.
- After you have completed this exercise, revise your I-Search paper by eliminating *there is/there are* sentence beginnings as directed in **Your Turn 8.**

PASSAGE A After watching a TV show about whale communication, I decided to find out how other animals communicate. I learned that ~~there are~~ some animals ~~that~~ "talk" to one another by sending vibrations through the ground. There is one type of mole rat that spends most of its life alone. There is a hammerlike sound it makes with its head on the ceiling of its burrow to avoid encountering other mole rats. There is also a special pattern of vibrations used by this type of mole rat to attract a mate. There are mole rats of the same species that know this sequence of vibrations and then find their way to the lonely suitor. There is no doubt that animal behavior is fascinating.

PASSAGE B There was a German composer and organist named Johann Sebastian Bach who lived from 1685 to 1750. There were 1,200 musical works written by Bach. Because I was fascinated by such a creative person, I decided to conduct further research. There were seventy-six musicians in his extended family. There were twenty children of Bach, four of whom became famous composers. There was a composition, called the *Two-Part Inventions,* that Bach wrote to train his children to play using each hand independent of the other.

Proofreading: Punctuating Titles

DIRECTIONS Proofread the following passage, correctly punctuating the titles, as shown in the passage.

- After you have completed this exercise, proofread your I-Search paper, and correct the punctuation of titles as directed in **Your Turn 9**.

Researching Dyslexia

Imagine being unable to learn the alphabet because you cannot remember the order of the letters. My brother, Lance, had that experience in kindergarten. Lance had dyslexia, a learning difficulty that affects writing, spelling, reading, listening, and speaking. I decided to gather some information of my own so that I could help my brother.

I began my search at a local college library, reading newspaper and magazine articles about dyslexia. The articles "Talk Back: My Experience with Dyslexia," in Personal History magazine; Ways to Teach Reading to Students with Dyslexia, in a periodical called Parent-Teacher Review; and How to Recognize Dyslexia, in our local newspaper, the Lumberville Gazette, were especially interesting. I also looked at the book Dyslexia: Solutions and Strategies, which included an informative chapter titled Learning Strategies for Dyslexics that offered practical suggestions for students with dyslexia. I then borrowed the library's copy of the film The Truth About Dyslexia and watched it twice at home. In addition, I watched an episode of the TV show Ask the Experts; the episode, which aired shortly after I began my research, was called Views on Dyslexia. After a lot of hard work by my brother and a little research by me, Lance overcame his dyslexia.

Journal Warm-up: Opinion Piece

Our school administrators should spend at least one day a year as students. They need to experience what we experience. They need to stand in cafeteria lines and strain to hear important announcements. They need to sit in classrooms and remember what it feels like to be a student. How else can they make informed decisions about school life?

Our local recycling center accepts only cans, newspapers, and transparent or white glass and plastic. Consequently, most of my family's trash is not recyclable. We need programs that teach people both how to reduce waste and how to dispose of all kinds of trash in imaginative, environmentally friendly ways.

JOURNAL STARTERS

Express and support an opinion by writing for five minutes, using one of these prompts.

- Do you think students should be allowed to attend classes at home via the Internet or go through home schooling? Why or why not?
- Many students are concerned about popularity at school. Do you believe popularity is important? Why or why not?
- Some schools have stopped offering art, music, and other classes because of budget cuts. Do you think these courses should be dropped? Why or why not?
- Should students be able to send and receive e-mail on computers at school? Why or why not?
- Many teenagers graduate from high school with little or no work experience. Should work experience be a high school graduation requirement? Why or why not?

NAME _______________ CLASS _______________ DATE _______________

Prewriting: Choosing an Issue and Developing Support

DIRECTIONS Use the graphic organizer below to help you develop your argument.

Issue:

Opinion Statement:

My Purpose:

My Audience:

- **Whom does this issue affect?**
- **Whom do I need to convince?**
- **Whom do I want to take action?**
- **Tone:**

Reasons People Should Agree with My Opinion	Evidence, Examples, Anecdotes	
	Logical Appeals	**Emotional Appeals**
1.		
2.		
3.		

NAME ______ CLASS ______ DATE ______

Eliminating Circular Reasoning

DIRECTIONS Ask the question *Why?* to determine whether the following passages use circular reasoning.

- Write *CR* on the line provided if the passage contains circular reasoning.
- Write *V* on the line if the reasoning is valid.

______ **1.** Property owners should look for alternative methods of dealing with deer because other ways of controlling deer are needed.

______ **2.** Because she is superior to everyone else running for office, our party's nominee is the best qualified of all the candidates.

______ **3.** The company sponsoring the team should supply the uniforms, since what the team wears is the company's responsibility.

______ **4.** Since it is well lit and easily patrolled by the police, the park should remain open to the public after sunset.

______ **5.** Taxes are too high because they cost taxpayers a lot of money.

______ **6.** Because it will be different from all the other businesses, a fast-food restaurant will change the character of the shopping area.

______ **7.** The fireworks display should be continued this year because it is an enjoyable event that brings everyone in the community together.

______ **8.** Since most club meetings and other after-school activities last longer than an hour, the buses should leave later in the afternoon.

______ **9.** The movie is popular because so many people like it.

______ **10.** A speaker from the senior class should be included in the graduation ceremony to share the seniors' perspective on their high school experience.

______ **11.** I was late for the game because I could not get to the field on time.

______ **12.** Because the painting is the only one of its kind in the world, there are no others like it.

______ **13.** The city is congested because it cannot handle all the traffic.

______ **14.** The north athletic fields are used more frequently because they are better maintained.

______ **15.** Her project received the most recognition because it won more awards than any of the others.

Writing: Writing Prompts

DIRECTIONS Choose your own issue for your persuasive paper, or use one of the following prompts.

CAREERS

Our society treats movie actors, athletes, and musicians as if they were heroes. Do you think they are worthy of this treatment? Why or why not? Imagine that you are a reporter commenting on this subject for a national news broadcast. Write a persuasive paper that states and supports your point of view.

SCHOOL

Some educators believe that all students should be required to pass a home economics course before graduating from high school. They argue that such courses teach basic life skills that everyone needs to know, such as cooking, sewing, and budgeting. Write a persuasive paper for your school newspaper stating and supporting your point of view on this topic.

JOURNALISM

Every day, editors all over the world decide which stories should or should not be covered in their newspapers. Are there subjects that are unacceptable for public newspapers? Should there be limits to freedom of the press for some topics? Write a persuasive paper for your local newspaper that answers each question.

SOCIAL STUDIES

The president of the United States employs many advisors who state and support their opinions. The president evaluates these opinions, analyzes the supporting information, and then decides on a course of action. If you were a presidential advisor, what opinion would you offer about a current policy or situation? What supporting facts and ideas would you provide for your opinion? Write a persuasive paper that summarizes and supports your views.

BIOLOGY

Many species of plants grow and thrive only after a fire has burned everything to the ground. Wildfires caused by lightning once burned forests and plains regularly, enabling these plant species to flourish. Some biologists believe that fires in national parks should be set deliberately to clear land and encourage new species to grow. Do you think this policy is wise or foolish? Write a persuasive paper that states and supports your opinion on this topic.

NAME CLASS DATE

Writing: Drafting Your Persuasive Paper

DIRECTIONS Complete the graphic organizer below, and use it to help you write your first draft. Use additional paper if necessary.

INTRODUCTION

- How will you capture your readers' attention?
- What background information will you provide?
- What is your opinion statement?

BODY

What is your first reason?	What is your second reason?	What is your third reason?
What evidence supports this reason?	What evidence supports this reason?	What evidence supports this reason?

CONCLUSION

- How will you restate your opinion?
- How will you summarize your reasons or include a call to action?

for **CHAPTER 27: YOUR TURN 6** ***page 789***

Revising: Persuasive Paper

DIRECTIONS Use this chart to help you improve your persuasive paper.

QUESTIONS	DO THIS	CHANGES YOU MADE
1. Does the introduction grab the audience's attention and include a clear opinion statement?	☐ **Bracket** attention-grabbing sentences. Revise if there isn't an attention grabber or an opinion statement. ☐ **Underline** opinion statement.	
2. Do at least three valid reasons support the opinion statement?	☐ **Number** reasons. Check for circular reasoning. If there is a problem, revise.	
3. Is each reason supported by at least one piece of evidence? If appropriate, are emotional appeals used?	☐ **Circle** evidence. ☐ **Draw arrows** from evidence to reasons.	
4. Are reasons and evidence arranged in order of importance?	☐ **Put a star** next to strongest reason.	
5. Does the conclusion restate the opinion and include a summary of reasons or a call to action?	☐ **Underline** summary. ☐ **Put a check mark** next to opinion restatement or call to action.	

for **CHAPTER 27: YOUR TURN 6** page 789

Revising Practice: Persuasive Paper

DIRECTIONS Below is an early draft of a persuasive paper.

- Revise the paper to make it more effective, using the guidelines on page 788.
- Look for problems with the introduction and support, and look for a missing reason.

Most people agree that it is important to save trees. I am one of those people.

Saving trees makes economic sense. Trees are also very important for beauty, shade, and shelter. An average tree sold as timber goes for about $600. That is a decent market price, but it is not much when you consider the cost over time. In contrast, the same tree, if allowed to grow for fifty years, is an excellent long-term investment. During its lifetime, a single tree produces about $200,000 of benefits to the environment. It provides oxygen, controls erosion, recycles water, curbs air pollution, enriches soil, and serves as a habitat for wildlife.

Revising: Evaluating Persuasive Papers

DIRECTIONS Use the following questions to evaluate your persuasive paper or that of one of your classmates.

- Answer the questions.
- Rate the parts of the paper. The lowest score is 1, and the highest is 4.
- Make at least three suggestions for improving the paper.

1. How does the introduction capture the reader's interest? What opinion is stated?	**Rating** 1 2 3 4 ***Suggestion:***
2. How many reasons are cited in support of the opinion? Are they all valid?	**Rating** 1 2 3 4 ***Suggestion:***
3. What evidence is used to support each reason? What kinds of emotional appeals are used, if any?	**Rating** 1 2 3 4 ***Suggestion:***
4. How effective is the arrangement of reasons and evidence? Does the arrangement indicate order of importance?	**Rating** 1 2 3 4 ***Suggestion:***
5. How effective is the conclusion in bringing the essay to a close through a summary or a call to action?	**Rating** 1 2 3 4 ***Suggestion:***

Eliminating Clichés

DIRECTIONS Revise each passage by replacing the clichés with original, more forceful phrases.

- First, underline the clichés. Then, cross out the words you need to replace, and write new phrases above them. You may delete or add other words if necessary.
- After you have completed this exercise, revise your persuasive essay to replace any clichés as directed in **Your Turn 7.**

PASSAGE A For centuries, poetry was passed down to audiences by word of mouth, not by silent paper pages. Ordinary people would lend their ears to the poets, who would combine speaking, acting, singing, and even dancing. Unfortunately, in time the printing press stole the show from poetry. After that, poetry just went downhill because it no longer brought people together in the same way. In all honesty, the tradition of performing poetry needs new life breathed into it, especially in the schools. In this day and age, students might jump for joy about poetry if they could experience creative, lively presentations of poems.

PASSAGE B It is crystal clear that visual media rule the roost with teenage students. Television, movies, and the World Wide Web are just a few of the many visual media that are in teenagers' faces on a daily basis. Teenagers need to learn how to evaluate, interpret, critique, and, if necessary, pull the plug on visual media information. Traditional scholastic resources—such as textbooks and library materials—are the cream of the crop because they are gone over with a fine-toothed comb before they see the light of day. In marked contrast, popular visual media seldom shoot straight and sometimes twist the truth.

Proofreading: Pronoun-Antecedent Agreement

DIRECTIONS Proofread the following passages.

- Underline the sentences that contain pronoun-antecedent agreement problems, and correct the errors.
- After you have completed this exercise, proofread your persuasive paper for errors in pronoun-antecedent agreement as directed in **Your Turn 8.**

PASSAGE A My friend Tony and other skateboarders are finding fewer and fewer safe places where he can skate. Tony's community has banned skateboarding on their streets, sidewalks, and parking lots. It's understandable. People don't like to see skateboarders rocketing toward them, and everyone worries about their children being injured. However, it seems a waste for security guards to spend his or her time stopping skateboarders. Just last week Tony and two other boys were skating in a vacant lot on South Street, and each of the boys got their skateboard taken away by a security guard. A community skate park is the solution to these problems.

PASSAGE B Every time I go to the park, someone has their outing ruined by an unleashed dog. Last weekend, I was walking on a path with my little sister and her friend Janey when two gigantic dogs charged up. Both my sister and Janey are very sure of herself, and I was not surprised when they began to swing at the dogs with their little backpacks. By the time the boys who owned them arrived, one of the dogs was fleeing with their tail tucked between their legs. Neither of the owners showed any concern about their responsibility to other people trying to use the park. Leash laws must be enforced; the city's parks were created for people, not for dogs!

NAME CLASS DATE

T.H.E.M.E.S. Strategy

DIRECTIONS The graphic organizer below shows six areas you might use to trigger ideas for reasons supporting your position.

- Choose one of the writing prompts below, and take a position on the issue.
- Then, write questions about how your position would affect the six categories below.
- Answer each of your questions. Your answers should give you reasons that support your opinion.

PROMPTS

- Some school districts are conducting school year-round. The year is divided into four segments, with a month's break between each. Imagine that you are going to address the school board, which is considering this schedule for your school. What is your position? What supporting reasons can you give?
- Breakfast provides energy to help you think well. Yet many students do not eat breakfast before coming to school each day. Could this situation be improved if the school cafeteria offered breakfast as well as lunch? What is your opinion on this issue? What supporting reasons can you give?

YOUR POSITION:

How Would Your Position Affect —

Time?

Health?

Education?

Money?

the Environment?

Safety?

Journal Warm-up: Critical Review

Maybe producers are finally noticing that viewers have brains! The new quiz show is a welcome change from the usual prime-time lineup. It has already attracted twice the viewers the network expected.

Commercials during TV news shows have a jarring effect. One minute viewers are looking at footage of a natural disaster, and the next minute they're singing along with the latest fast-food commercial.

Screenwriters need a reality check. The latest movies are way behind TV shows in showing life as it really is. For example, women on TV work, take care of their kids, do chores at home, and maintain personal interests. In contrast, women in recent films don't seem to have jobs to go to or anything in particular to do.

JOURNAL STARTERS

Write about your opinions of television for five minutes, using one of these prompts.

- Persuade a friend to watch your favorite TV show.
- Tell a family member why you would like to switch channels to a different show.
- Explain to someone younger than you why he or she should not watch a particular show.
- Write to a TV network, suggesting a change in its programming.
- Persuade a teacher to allow your class to view a particular TV show.

Prewriting: Reviewing Your Sitcom

DIRECTIONS Complete the organizer below to help you plan your review.

Name of Sitcom I Will Review:

My Purpose:	My Audience:	My Tone:
		My Voice:

REVIEWING LOG

Elements of a Sitcom	Questions Based on Evaluation Criteria	My Responses
Plot	Does the plot hold my attention? Is it funny? Is it original? Are conflicts believable?	
Characters	Are the characters realistic? funny? sympathetic? Do they learn and change? Do they play off each other well?	
Acting	Are the actors believable and consistent? Are they fun to watch?	
Writing	Are the scenes funny and believable? Is dialogue natural?	
Theme	Are the themes relevant to viewers?	

Evaluating Support

DIRECTIONS Evaluate the support in each of the following items.

- Write *S* on the line if the item contains strong support.
- Write *W* on the line if the support in the item is weak.
- Be prepared to explain your answers.

______ **1.** The sitcom *An Apple a Day* is both humorous and informative. It shows how medical personnel look on the bright side to reduce the stress of working in a hospital emergency room.

______ **2.** I do not recommend the sitcom *My Life as a Superstar.* It is totally unrealistic! No one would believe what happens on the show.

______ **3.** You could call the 1970s the decade of bionics on TV. First, a show called *The Six Million Dollar Man* depicted the life of a man who was part machine, part human. Then, *The Bionic Woman,* another program about bionics, captured viewers' attention. The Bionic Woman even had a bionic dog!

______ **4.** TV news stories are not original. They come from the newspaper. That is why I do not watch TV newscasts. I read the newspaper instead.

______ **5.** *Monday Night Jokefest* is the funniest show I have ever seen. The constant stream of hilarious jokes and pranks keeps me laughing from the beginning of the show to the end.

______ **6.** TV commercials make a powerful impression on viewers. For example, most children in the United States can sing the jingle from their favorite TV commercial but have a hard time remembering the words to the national anthem.

______ **7.** Watching the news is a passive activity. Many viewers just sit back, look at the images, and let the newscaster shape their ideas about people and events in the news.

______ **8.** Do not even think of watching this show. It is amazing that it is allowed on the air. Who is responsible for this awful program?

______ **9.** If you rely on TV sitcoms for your ideas about the world, you are in serious trouble. These shows may make you laugh, but they do not depict reality.

______ **10.** This season's newest sitcom should be an instant hit with younger viewers. Many teens will identify with the show's main characters, Denard and Tina, and their experiences at Liverpool High School.

NAME CLASS DATE

for **CHAPTER 28: YOUR TURN 6** *page 819*

Prewriting: Getting Ready to Write

DIRECTIONS Follow these steps before moving on to the writing stage.

- Write a thesis that states your opinion and the basic reasons for it.
- Use the chart below to gather support for your reasons.
- Draw a graphic organizer to plan the organization of your ideas. You may use the organizer on page 819 as a model.

THESIS STATEMENT

SUPPORT CHART

ELEMENT	REASONS	SUPPORT
Plot		
Characters		
Acting		
Writing		
Theme		

ORGANIZATION

GRAPHIC ORGANIZER

Writing: Writing Prompts

DIRECTIONS Choose a television program for your critical review, or use one of the following prompts.

CAREERS

List jobs held by characters in TV shows that you watch on a regular basis. Select one of the careers that interests you, and find out more about it at the library, on the Internet, or by talking with someone who has a similar career. Then, watch several episodes of the TV show, and pay special attention to how the career is portrayed. Write a critical review, focusing on one aspect of the show.

SCHOOL

Your school broadcasts television newscasts and other programs specifically for students. Because the programming contains commercials, however, your state is considering banning TVs from the classroom. Write a review of one of your favorite school TV programs in the form of a letter to the state department of education, expressing your views of the program and the effect of the commercials.

BIOLOGY

Your friends are always talking about the latest episodes of their favorite sitcoms. The TV in your home, however, is always set to the channel that features nature shows. Write a review of an episode of one of these shows to persuade your friends to switch to that channel once in a while.

HISTORY

Many historians are concerned about the popularity of docudramas, which use a story line based on actual events but weave in fictional dialogue and scenes. Docudramas have focused on everything from Civil War battles to contemporary murder cases, and they often combine newsreel footage with segments in which actors dramatize events. Why do you think historians are worried about docudramas? Write a critical review of this type of TV show for your local newspaper's television section. In your review, identify and respond to the concerns.

ART

The public television network is sponsoring a series about art. Every week the network's art critic visits one of the world's great art museums and highlights some of the artwork on exhibit. You found the series fascinating. Write a letter to the show's producer in the form of a critical review of the series, expressing your enthusiasm.

for **CHAPTER 28: YOUR TURN 7** *page 820*

Writing: Drafting Your Critical Review

DIRECTIONS Complete the graphic organizer below, and use it to help you write your first draft. Use additional paper if necessary.

INTRODUCTION

- How will you grab the audience's attention?
- What background information will you provide?
- What is your thesis?

BODY

What is your first reason?	Observations/Examples:
What is your second reason?	Observations/Examples:
What is your third reason?	Observations/Examples:

CONCLUSION

- How will you restate your opinion in the form of a recommendation?
- How will you close your review?

for **CHAPTER 28: YOUR TURN 8** *page 825*

Revising: Critical Review

DIRECTIONS Use this chart to help you improve your critical review.

QUESTIONS	DO THIS	CHANGES YOU MADE
1. Does the introduction grab the audience's attention?	☐ **Underline** attention-grabbing sentences.	
2. Does the introduction contain an opinion statement and a list of reasons?	☐ **Highlight** the opinion statement and reasons.	
3. Does each body paragraph present a reason?	☐ **Circle** key words that signal a reason.	
4. Does each body paragraph provide support?	☐ **Bracket** observations and examples.	
5. Does the organization help the review's effectiveness?	☐ **Number** body paragraphs in order of importance as support for the opinion.	
6. Is the opinion restated as a recommendation in the conclusion?	☐ **Put a check mark** next to any sentence that restates the opinion.	

Revising Practice: Critical Review

DIRECTIONS Below is an early draft of a critical review.

- Revise the review to make it more effective, using the guidelines on page 824.
- Look for problems with the opener, an opinion statement and reasons supporting it, and lack of observations and examples to support evaluation.

Antonio Perez plays Pete, one of the main characters of *Dads and Daughters*. Pete is a widower raising four daughters. His brother, Irving, is played by renowned actor Alex O'Rourke. Irving is a professional chef. Irv's best friend, Alan, played by character actor Hal Henderson, is a sports coach. Irv and Alan are around the house so much the girls think of them as extra dads. Irv and Alan pitch in with help in every way they can, doing dishes and dishing out advice.

The talented cast makes this creative situation come alive. Twins Marta and Maria Estefan share the role of the youngest daughter, Desiree.

NAME CLASS DATE

Revising: Evaluating Critical Reviews

DIRECTIONS Use the following questions to evaluate your critical review or that of one of your classmates.

- Answer the questions.
- Rate the parts of the review. The lowest score is 1, and the highest is 4.
- Make at least three suggestions for improving the review.

1. What grabs the reader's attention in the opening sentences?	**Rating** 1 2 3 4 ***Suggestion:***
2. What opinion is stated in the introduction? Are reasons provided?	**Rating** 1 2 3 4 ***Suggestion:***
3. Does each body paragraph present a reason based on criteria for evaluating television programs?	**Rating** 1 2 3 4 ***Suggestion:***
4. What observations and examples support the evaluation in each body paragraph?	**Rating** 1 2 3 4 ***Suggestion:***
5. How does the review's organization contribute to its effectiveness?	**Rating** 1 2 3 4 ***Suggestion:***
6. How does the conclusion restate the writer's opinion?	**Rating** 1 2 3 4 ***Suggestion:***

Combining Sentences Using Adverb Clauses

DIRECTIONS Revise each passage by using adverb clauses to combine simple sentences that are related in meaning.

- You may delete or add words if necessary.
- After you have completed this exercise, revise your review by using adverb clauses to combine closely related simple sentences into longer, complex sentences as directed in **Your Turn 9**.

PASSAGE A The average American youth devotes almost a third of his or her waking hours to watching TV. Children watch a total of 5,000 hours of TV. This is before they begin first grade. The average American teenager has watched a lot of TV by the time he or she graduates from high school. The average teen has watched 19,000 hours of TV by then. School is more important than TV. That same teenager will have been in school for only 13,000 hours by graduation. That many hours of watching TV must have a negative effect on young people. The TV viewing of young people should be limited.

PASSAGE B We should bear in mind that TV news programs are shows. One of their major goals is to entertain viewers. Consider all the elements of a successful TV news broadcast. They are not much different from those of a theater production. The newscast is introduced by a snappy musical theme. People respond to catchy tunes. The news broadcast showcases seemingly responsible, good-looking anchors. This makes viewers keep watching. Heartwarming human-interest stories are strategically placed. They establish a false sense of intimacy. TV news programs are shows that are meant to entertain us so that we will watch commercials and spend our money on advertisers' products.

Proofreading: Run-On Sentences

DIRECTIONS Proofread the passage below.

- Revise by eliminating run-on sentences. Correct each run-on sentence by using one of the methods described on page 829.
- After you have completed this exercise, proofread and correct your review for run-on sentences as directed in **Your Turn 10.**

Brown Thumbs

The TV sitcom *The Grass Is Always Greener* delightfully reverses viewers' expectations. On this show about a professional landscaper, plants in perfect health get sick, plants that are already ill get worse. The star of the series, Jim Green, is always experimenting with his customers' yards for no reason other than fun they don't always see it that way. Once, he put a herd of goats on the grass, expecting that they would eat and trim it just like a mower would to his surprise they chewed up all the bushes and ignored the lawn. Then, instead of fertilizing the grass, he sprayed it with green paint, the entire lawn died from the stress.

Green tackles his character with relaxed good humor he shows he can laugh at himself. His role is complicated, he makes it seem easy. Green actually acts in a show within the show, his character is the host of a fictional TV program called *Green Thumbs*. Green's sitcom wife, Serena, sees his "experiments" with a clear eye, she forgives his many huge mistakes. She is not as easygoing when he experiments with their own yard later she usually laughs along with Jim and the TV audience. Viewers might not get any tips on how to improve their yards from this charming sitcom, the show probably will improve their moods!